ZOOM FOR BEGINNERS

Learn how to manage your classroom correctly, thanks to zoom cloud meetings. Make webinars, live streams, and conferences easy even if you start from scratch.

MICHELLE HARRIS

TABLE OF CONTENTS

INTRODUCTION   5

CHAPTER - 1
WHAT IS ZOOM?   15

CHAPTER - 2
DIFFERENT BETWEEN ZOOM AND
OTHER SIMILAR APPS   19

CHAPTER - 3
GETTING STARTED WITH ZOOM   33

CHAPTER - 4
STARTING YOUR CLASS IN ZOOM
BY STARTING A MEETING   49

CHAPTER - 5
HOW TO PRESENT YOURSELF IN
VIDEO CHAT WITH YOUR
STUDENTS   55

CHAPTER - 6
FREE ZOOM VS PAID ZOOM   61

CHAPTER - 7
HOW TO USE ZOOM TO
TEACH MATH   65

CHAPTER - 8

HOW TO USE THE WHITEBOARD IN
ZOOM   73

CHAPTER - 9

HOW TO MAKE STUDENTS
UNDERSTAND THAT A LESSON
ON ZOOM IS LIKE A REAL
CLASSROOM LESSON   79

CHAPTER - 10

HOW TO BE AN INNOVATIVE
TEACHER ON ZOOM   85

CHAPTER - 11

HOW TO GET THE STUDENTS'
CONCENTRATION THROUGHOUT
THE LESSON   93

CHAPTER - 12

HOW NOT TO GET CHEATED
DURING THE TESTS   97

CHAPTER - 13

TIPS & TRICKS   107

CHAPTER - 14

MOST CRUCIAL SETTINGS
IN ZOOM   123

CONCLUSION

143

INTRODUCTION

When the planet is turned into a digital community, online forums, webinars, and conferences become the buzzwords of the day. Since globalization is touching the farthest reaches of the planet, Web forums, electronic events, and web-based meetings have taken on different dimensions. Conferences often used to be held with a variety of fanfare before using online or video meeting techniques.

In the past, the presence of the Chairman of an international shore company was a remarkable event. The branch office at home can fly two weeks before it leaves and offers it a major welcome right at the airport. For the president exiting the limo and reaching the building, a red carpet will be rolled out, and a widely known ceremony will be conducted in the memory of the leader where anyone can function. Such things have vanished since online conferences were introduced. Today top executives only attend regional offices when they are completely required. Everything is done by video conferencing now. Online events are also holding educational workshops, discussions, and seminars. WebEx is the most common web conference platform by far. It allows you 'to offer IT service to dispersed workers in real-time.' This also lets you 'reduce downtime while optimizing efficiency for helpdesks.'

Virtual meetings or cloud sessions, which are often named, are the specialized technological counterpart to a conventional conference. Many individuals going to the same location at once to address the statistics and figures or any important details have often been interested in typical meetings. The number of journeys one or more of these people can create to meet a typical conference maybe thousands of kilometers on a plane, hundreds of powered miles or both. It sums up to a great deal of effort and money that would be avoided otherwise.

You can meet anytime and at any time with just a computer, an Internet link, and a password. There are several various businesses on the internet that will give you both fees per minute and services to manage the business meetings, which allows you to access their apps, which monitors and integrates the meetings and help you chat, exchange information, and validate ideas together in real-time. During an online conference, you will use visuals, music, text, and video to get the details you need to exchange. If you can do all that, you can save your business a great deal of money in expense, make your business greener, and save time on profitability.

In this sense, you can see why drawing a modern technologically advanced online meeting, which, in contrast to a conventional meeting, is more realistic in any way. Based on the number of conventional meetings your organization organizes, the money your business will save using the latest and enhanced electronic meeting system would depend on the volume. Reducing your carbon footprint is indeed something the organization will confidently use to affirm its reputation. The loss of gasoline or electricity decreases the carbon footprint; it helps the organization involved to conserve not only capital but also precious resources. The profitability of companies has, therefore, improved because less time has spent commuting from location to position; the bureau is moved to the area in which decisions are made. The decisions made during an electronic meeting should be applied instantly so that the company is less time-out, and change is lost in this specific field.

It may be challenging to determine which organization you're going to use to hold your online meeting, as many organizations provide web resources to satisfy your web needs. Until choosing which organization you should choose to hold your meetings, ensure that you evaluate that services, quality of support, consumer feedback, and costs.

What is Video Conferencing?

Video conferencing is a communications technology that combines voice and video to connect remote users over the internet in the same place. For each participant to engage in a video conference, a device, microphone, webcam, and broadband Internet access are needed. Users see and hear each other at both ends in real-time to make a normal conversation. Many media firms have become interested in the application of video conferencing.

For high-quality video conferencing, reasonable bandwidth is needed. The launching of the Microsoft Net meeting rendered video conferences more famous. There are already a variety of organizations selling apps for video conferencing.

Video conferencing is very appealing for education and business. Video conferences allowed users to be near (virtually face-to-face) while saving time and energy. Video conferencing has been embraced by several institutions as an instructional resource. Worldwide, businesses use video conferencing to stay in contact with others.

Virtual conferences are in a more challenging process, and more software and technologies for video conferencing are being built and enhanced. Finally, video conferences would allow the creation of virtual communities, remote locations where people can function together without needing to be on the same premises physically. A video conference service may be built using a device, a video camera, and a broadband internet link.

Video conferencing is a very convenient form of communicating as it will save citizens time and travel expenses. A video conference between two is referred to as point-to-point and is regarded as a multi-point conference among the more men. In addition to visual and audio communications between persons, video conferencing is often utilized for the exchange of data, electronic knowledge viewed.

Distance Learning

Video conferencing is used by educators in primary, secondary, and higher education and corporate training. Video tutorials become a common occurrence. There are many applications in the classroom that digitally take remote visitors and offer essential lectures. There are wonderful possibilities to render the schooling cycle more efficient by video conferencing.

Why is Video Conferencing Necessary in Developing Countries?

If we speak of video conferencing, developed nations all over the world will benefit from it. We now see the effects of video conferencing in the newspapers, governments, and businesses in all the big metropolitan centers, and have achieved impressive results. Throughout the developed world, we find that all the facilities they like are conveniently available throughout metro cities that have a rather large literacy rate. Yet it's not the same in remote regions. When we consider certain individuals, who are willing to train themselves on some modern technologies but lack the opportunities. Knowledge in villages is relevant since construction in all areas in rural and urban areas should be standardized. The invention of satellite television has changed society revolutionarily and has shown that animation has a broader impact to sensitize and inform citizens. Video conferencing should be used as a method for dramatic improvements in production in rural areas.

Why Video Conferencing is Becoming so Popular

Let us look at this from a very broad perspective by trying to look at the need base and the current reality - this will enable us to rationalize why video conferencing has become the new norm. It was never a new endeavor. The idea of video conferencing dated far back as 20th century, when the first ever video conference held in 1964 - about 50years ago. The wake of technological advancements in the 21st century has given more power to video conferencing with the advent of powerful video cameras and sophisticated computers.

The latter part of 2019 saw the world waking up to the new reality, as the pandemic extended his tentacles sweeping across our planet. Much hope was in the air, with optimism, from all quarters that the pandemic will be contained much more quickly than it came. Even aliens in the world shared in this naive optimism. Currently, in the first half of the year 2020, the pandemic seems like what has come to stays forever. While much of the activities across the whole world have been put on hold, with people staying far away from their workplace, market places and schools, it, then becomes imperative to carry on with our lives even in the face of the global shutdown. At a period like this, video conferencing has dominated our space, giving us a unique opportunity to do what we have otherwise been doing before. Schools, corporate spaces, political institutions and other platforms have been leveraging hugely on video conferencing to schedule meetings, meet expectations and carry on with classes. Video conferencing today, more than ever before, brings all the components of computers and electronic technology together to give us a feeling that is today the closest reality anyone can relate with.

While it is gaining popularity by the day, let's explore some of the other reasons video conferencing has fitted into part of our everyday life.

1. Internet connectivity today has become extremely affordable, with almost all the countries of the world having access to basic internet. According to trusted reports, web access in the United States has reached over 80%, with businesses taking advantage of this to increase their presence and promote their businesses using online media platforms. With faster and affordable internet access, businesses can save money by way of conference video- where they can connect and hold meetings with clients- this saves cost of transportation to business meetings. The risk of accidents while attending business meetings is in fact reduced now

that businesses can come online.

2. A web camera is the ingredient of an effective video meeting. Now, with advancement integrated into smartphones, Mac and Windows, we can have smartphones fitted with great cameras for proper video calls. Web cameras can now, even, be fitted into our laptops and tablets, all for the sole purpose of making an enhanced video. With a great camera, you can have a successful video conference.

3. With video conferencing, we can now bring our classrooms and seminars online. Students can participate actively in learning while at the comfort of their houses.

4. Video conferencing is a new way of being with people you love without necessarily having a physical presence. Couples, in time past, have used video conferencing platforms for their wedding and needless to say, it is very effective and less time-consuming.

If there is something this global pandemic is teaching the world right now, it is that we can go on with our activities seamlessly even while at the comfort of our rooms. All thanks to video conferencing platforms.

CHAPTER - 1

What is Zoom?

Zoom is a virtual conferencing platform that is easy to use.

Historical Background of Zoom

Zoom Video Communication, Inc. (Zoom) was founded in the year 2011, April 21 by Eric Yuan a Chinese indigene, and its headquarter is located in San Jose, California. Eric Yuan was a former corporate vice president of Cisco WebEx who left the company to start his own company when his idea to create a smartphone-friendly conferencing system in cisco. While he was leaving, he left with 40 engineers to start his own company which was originally named SaaS bee, Inc. before it was later changed to Zoom in September 2012.

At the start of the company, they had financial difficulties because no one was willing to invest in the company. In the long run, Zoom was able to raise $3million to fund its business from some organizations like WebEx, General Counsel, and Venture capitalists in June 2011.

In September 2012, Zoom launched a beta version of its application which could host video conferencing calls with 15 participants. Zoom signed Stanford University as its first customer in November 2012.

In the year 2013, Eric Yuan launched the Zoom software service where he was able to raise $6million. with version 1.0 of the Zoom application being launched, the numbers of participants for the video conferencing increase from 15 to 25, and by the end of the month, zoom users increased to 400,000, and by May 2013, it had 1 million users.

Zoom Is the Future

Okay now let's get down to the business, the main idea behind using Zoom for audio and video meeting is connecting and supporting people from a distance. Think of it as your virtual meeting room online and you and many people or you and just one person can actually have a real meeting. There are so many benefits to using zoom as a meeting platform.

Better Communication - You can see the people's reactions their facial and non-verbal expressions. Everything is much better than talking on the phone. It's a much better way of doing it, it's more productive people are right at their desk or in their home and they're able to get work done.

Saves Time and Travel Time - You can have a working meeting at any time, and you and your team can work maybe on a spreadsheet or a document together. It works great and it also saves a lot of time travel, so you don't have to travel for one place to another. You can just get on the meeting and when you get off the meeting, you're right there being productive again.

Participants Can Control Their Involvement – One great thing about Zoom meetings is that the participants have a lot of control over how involved they are in the meeting and you'll find that sometimes people are more involved in an online meeting because they're able to interact constantly with themselves with the presenter and with each other.

In addition to a Zoom subscription, Zoom Rooms allow additional subscriptions and are a perfect option for larger companies.

CHAPTER - 2

Different Between Zoom and Other Similar Apps

Zoom Vs. Other Conferencing Tools

For remote teams, the most preferred collaboration devices are the Zoom, Skype, Facebook rooms, Google Hangouts, Microsoft Teams, ezTalks, Cisco Webex, and BlueJeans etc.

All these platforms can be used to hold video calls, chat, and host meetings or webinars. And if you're looking for a new platform to help you do these things, you're probably considering platforms like these.

Ultimately, the variations between all of them may not seem significant. But the decision to implement one over another can still impact your team significantly. It's easy to say from the experiences of a remote team that every platform fits different needs, and that is why it is important to your decision to understand the pros and cons, features and pricing, etc.

Zoom Vs. Facebook Rooms

Facebook has finally revealed what its Zoom competitor, Messenger Quarters, can be renamed. The video calling application is integrated into the standalone Facebook Messenger app and is intended for personal use. In comparison, Zoom is based on technical video conferencing. But since both are end-of-day video calling apps, here is a comparison based on functionality, quality of the web, and more.

1. Availability

Both are present in iOS and android when it comes to availability and have a web edition that can be obtained from anywhere. This means you can reach it on Windows OS, as well as on macros and ChromeOS. What's more, you don't have to download a separate Messenger Rooms app, as it's built into the Messenger app itself.

2. Free or Not

You do not have to pay for any of the features in Zoom as you do. While Zoom also has a free tier, most of its features are restricted to the paid edition. Zoom has three paid plans costing $14.99 a month, and $19.99 a month. However, up to 100 participants are still in favor of the free version.

3. Characteristics

In this one, Zoom gets an edge as the video conferencing application can support up to 100 participants in one call session. The paid version can support up to 350: participants, and even 500. Though, at the moment, Facebook Messenger Rooms are limited to 50 participants.

Yet when it comes to video call size, Messenger Rooms is taking the lead. It allows you to speak with 50 people for unlimited minutes at a time, while Zoom's free tier can support 100 (or less) participants in a 40-minute call. The paid version can tolerate calls up to 24 hours.

Since Zoom is designed for organizational use, it also has the function of call recording, and something is missing from Messenger Room right now. The biggest advantage of Facebook is the audience that it already has in the main app and the Messenger app. Using News Feed, Groups, and Events, you can start and share rooms on Facebook, and it's comfortable for people to drop by.

Facebook says it will quickly add ways to create Instagram Direct, WhatsApp, and Portal rooms. Though both offer you the versatility to communicate text during a video call and share screens with others.

Skype Vs. Zoom

Several applications for video conferencing are on the market. Skype is among the competition's largest and oldest brands. It allows single-to-one video calls, instant messaging, screen sharing, group calls, and file sharing, much like Zoom.

Skype redirects messages to an email inbox for those who participate offline. Skype is still lagging behind its competition, though, in that the platform only allows up to ten participants at a time. A no-go definitely for larger conferences.

According to Global Industry Forecasts, video conferencing is expected to become a 20-million-dollar industry by the end of 2024.

Below is a comparison of Zoom vs. Skype's features, pricing, and product performance to secure the best video conferencing needs.

Overview Zoom vs. Skype

Zoom

It's an innovative cloud-based with modern conference tools. Zoom derives with breakout sessions that can be used to divide your viewers (e.g., customers or employees) into small groups for like webinar training, specific topics, or some online class discussions.

The organizer has the power to monitor the meeting to the full with Zoom. You can also mute all microphones when not in use, watch presentation access for the attendants, and so on. Besides, this method allows the participants to participate by digitally raising their hands to the discussion.

The chat utility of Zoom also allows viewers to communicate directly with your instructor and with other participants, thus ensuring a collective classroom setup.

Skype

Imagine communicating with your employees directly from your PC / phone through instant short messaging service, screen sharing, file sharing, and informal or formal audio or video calls. Effective and direct, that's all about Skype.

Skype is designed to make simple communication using revolutionary technology. Its intuitive chat interface, like Zoom, allows users to send prompt messages to other users. Users can integrate video with audio from their chat windows without any effort.

General Information

When considering Skype vs. Zoom, the biggest challenge is that they are both very powerful channels of communication. Deciding between these two can be difficult, as both are efficient and cost-effective.

By definition, a Zoom is a software-based on video or audio conferencing that was intended to promote collaboration through an advanced integrated system with featuring web conferences, group messaging, and important online meetings.

On the opposite hand, Skype provides powerful tools for text, voice, and video, providing users with a smart way to share the experiences with others, no matter where they are.

1. Devices

Zoom supports Web platforms such as Android, iPhone, Mac, iPad.

Web-based Skype supports all Windows, Android, and iPhones.

Zoom is filled with a variety of features, including video conferences, streamlined scheduling, and collaboration between groups. This platform's other powerful features include local and cloud recording in premium audio feature, and in Zoom Meetings and Zoom Rooms.

Skype also comes with powerful chat tools, including Skype-to-Skype calls, community calls, call-forwards, one-to-one video calls, and instant messaging. You can send and exchange emails, video messages, displays, files, and contacts.

2. Clients

Zoom and Skype both deliver premium video conferencing solutions — a factor they have loyal customers around the globe.

3. Designed for

Both Zoom and Skype are perfect for the small businesses to significant business, but freelancers are also popular with Skype's free plan.

4. Pricing

Zoom offers four pricing packages for enterprises: Zoom Basic Plan, Zoom Pro Plan, Zoom Business Plan, and Zoom Enterprise Plan.

Basic Plan

The basic package — which is explicitly tailored for personal meetings — is free, can host up to 100 people, and provides one-on-one sessions without restrictions. It's an excellent gratuitous bid. You will use this program to:

- Team of conducts meets for up to forty minutes

- Have a plethora of meetings

- Get the support online

- Enjoy the functions of web and video

conferencing

- Make sure community collaboration is safe

Zoom Pro Plan

It is for the small teams, and it costs $14.99 per user per month. It comes with all the basic plan functionality and can accommodate 100 participants.

This program also includes business interoperability user management tools, admin controls, REST API, and Skype. Users can store and share large amounts of data with 1GB data of mp4 and m4a Cloud recording.

The optional Zoom add-on plans

This include five sub-plans:

- $40 a month for extra cloud recording storage.

- $49 per month for 323/ SIP Room Connector.

- $49 a month for joining Zoom Rooms.

- $100 a month for toll-free dialing / Call Me.

- $40 a month for adding video webinars.

Business Plan

The business strategy for the zoom, which is worth $19.99 a month per user, is limited to smaller businesses. Equipped with all the Pro plan's functionality, mid-sized companies will use it to take their connectivity to another level.

The plan lets you host up to 10 hosts, it has an admin control dashboard, telephone support, and a vanity URL. The Business Plan is an excellent option if you prefer on-premise placement than certain characteristics of the scheme include:

- Manage domains and one-way sign-on
- Client branding and customized emails
- Integration with LTI

Zoom Plan for Enterprise

Zoom Enterprise is for $19.99 per person/host per month. In this plan, which includes all the Business Plan features which needs you to have a minimum of 100 hosts. Up to 200 participants are allowed into this plan.

The Enterprise package is ideal for large organizations with diverse meeting needs, with unrestricted cloud storage, a zealous client service manager, and executive company feedback.

Skype

Skype is free of charge. Anyhow, if you're looking to improve efficiency and increase revenue, Skype has a $2-per-month enterprise price package per user.

Business Plan

For Skype's Business Plan, users can use solid authentication as well as encryption to enjoy features like online meetings (250 participants) and secure communication lines.

Online Plan 2

This plan costs $5.50 a month per user and is designed for online business meetings. You can use Online Plan 2 to:

Join any Equipment

- Enjoy HD video in the group as well as audio calling (for 250 people)

- Receive mobile technical assistance at the client level

- Office versions available online

- 50 GB Postbox

- 1 TB Store File

Office 365 Professional Premium

This plan is for $12.50 per user per month. The Office 365 Company Critical plan has notable features, including:

- Government software pre-installed on PC / Mac

- Tablet and mobile apps

- In addition, Microsoft's parent company Skype has supported Microsoft Teams over Skype as a forum for meeting and video conferencing. As a result, Skype support may diminish in favor of Teams over time.

Backend Integrations Zoom

Zoom supports

- Microsoft One Drive

- Salesforce Box

- Slack

- Okta

- Microsoft Outlook

- LTI (Canvas, Desire2Learn, Backboard and Moodle)

- Google Chrome

- Marketo

- Facebook Centrify

- Intel Unite

- Kubi

- Zapier

- RSA

Other integrations that Zoom supports include:

- Google Drive, DropBox, Pardot
- Firefox and Acuity Calendar
- Eloqua and the Microsoft Active Directory
- Hipchat, Infusionsoft, and HubSpot

Skype

Provides integration with such programs as:

- Office (Word, Lync, Outlook, PowerPoint)
- WordPress
- Mendix
- Lucid Meetings
- OnePage CRM
- Bitium
- Cayzu Helpdesk
- BigContacts
- SalesExec
- Interactive Intelligence CaaaS
- 1CRM
- Grasshopper
- Slack
- GroupWise

Skype can also be integrated with other systems, such as:

- CRM Agile

- Wimi and 88 Center for Virtual Touch

- Microsoft Dynamics Online CRM

- The Concierge and Yugma Moxie

- Zoom vs. Skype: The Low Line

Zoom and Skype both deliver customized solutions and are designed to take interactions from your company/class to the next level. But the free and paid third-party enhancements apps enhance Zoom and give it a slight edge.

CHAPTER - 3

Getting Started with Zoom

How to Download and Install it on Your PC

With more people starting to work in most sectors from home, remote conferencing technology has never been more relevant. Services such as Zoom, which offer online meetings and video calls, become more critical than ever to help businesses run smoothly while physical offices are closed.

Fortunately, installing Zoom to your PC is a quick process that will get you up and running in just a few minutes with the service. While you need to sign up for a free account to use zoom, you'll be able to use it immediately once the program is installed on your computer.

Here is how you can download Zoom to your PC.

STEP - 01

Open the internet browser on your computer, and link to the Zoom.us website.

STEP - 02

Scroll down to the bottom of the page, and in the footer of the web page, click "Download."

STEP - 03

Click "Download" on the Download Center page under the section called "Zoom Client for Meetings."

NS ▾   PLANS & PRICING   CONTACT SALES   JOIN A MEETING   HOST A MEETING

Download Center   Download for IT A

Zoom Client for Meetings

The web browser client will download automatically when you start or join your first Zoom meeting, and is also available for manual download here.

Download   Version 4.6.7 (18176.0301)

STEP - 04

You will then start installing the Zoom app. To begin the installation process, you can then click on the .exe file.

When enabled, you'll need to log into your Zoom account, which can be set up via the Zoom website if you don't have one already. If developed, you can use Zoom to meet all your video calls and online needs as usual.

Registration

If you intend to use your personal computer or laptop, you need to go to the official Zoom website (https://zoom.us/freesignup) and register by entering the requested data.

Now choose one of the two options:

- Manual registration: by entering the email address and confirming registration.

- Register by link from our Google or Facebook account

The next step is to install the Zoom client on your computer. To do this, go to https://zoom.us/download and download "Zoom".

Audio and Video Control

It's important you learn the control for audio and video if you want to use Zoom efficiently. If you want to find these controls, look in the lower left corner of the screen. The icon more to the left is the control for Audio while the one next to it with the icon of a video camera is for Video.

If both icons are turned off, you'll see them having a red line going across them. So, if you're on a video call, the other person will not be able to see you or hear what you're saying

STEP - 01

To enable audio, click the Audio icon on the far left once. The microphone will show a green icon to signify that it can receive audio. If you want to mute yourself again, press the icon once again and it will be muted.

STEP - 02

If you want to enable video, click the Video icon beside the Audio icon. Your webcam will turn on and the other person will be able to see you. Press the icon once again to disable Video

Enhancing Video Quality

One of the features that made Zoom to be unique is the ability to do video conference and it will be so bad if the host and participants using Zoom during a meeting are unable to enjoy good video quality. To get to the bottom of this, follow the instructions below

STEP - 01

When you open your Zoom, application click on settings at the right-hand side

STEP - 02

Click on video

STEP - 03

Click on enable HD

STEP - 04

Click on touch my appearance

STEP - 05

Click on turn off video when joining a meeting

STEP - 06

See illustrations below for clearer understanding

Enhancing the Audio Quality

To have a good quality audio sound when having a meeting, follow the following instructions

When you open your Zoom application click on settings at the right-hand side

STEP - 01

Click on audio

STEP - 02

Test the speaker to see if it works properly

STEP - 03

Test the microphone to ensure it is working

STEP - 04

You can also adjust the volume to your taste

STEP - 05

You can also go to advance settings to suppress background noise and intermediate noise

See the images below for clarity

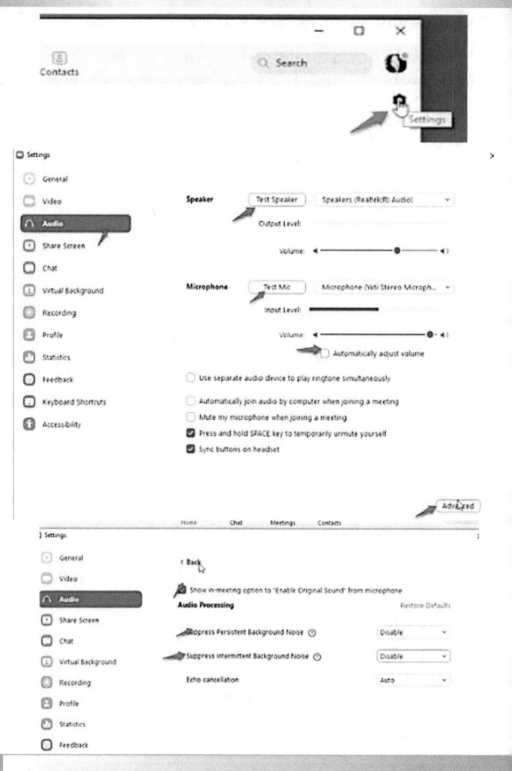

Verification of Those Who Present

When you log in to Zoom and start a call, you'll only be able to see the person talking at the moment. If there is no audio coming from the other participants, they won't appear fully on the screen. This is because Zoom can identify who the active speaker is and the other people who are muted.

If another participant were to speak, the audio will be detected automatically, and the camera will then switch and show them on the screen. But if you're in a meeting with others, one great feature you would love is the Gallery view.

You'll find this at the top right-hand corner. With this feature enabled, you'll be able to see everyone connected to the meeting. On one screen, you can only see 49 people at once. And you can toggle that on in the Settings. This is very helpful as seeing everyone at once gives that feeling of being connected, plus you'll know if someone has questions or isn't paying attention.

Another important feature is the Manage Participants options along the lower toolbar. You'll notice 4 icons, when you select the box, a window will pop up on the right side. The Host of the meeting will be able to Manage Participants.

Those joining the meeting also have the Participants option but it's only to see the rest of the people that have joined the meeting. The host will be shown at the top and this is so that other participants can find the host easily

At the bottom of the screen, you'll find the button for Mute All which you'll need if there's noise coming from different participants. You can also remove permission for others to unmute themselves if things get to that point.

You can also hover on a participant and you'll find a dropdown. The first on the list is the Chat option to chat privately. If there's anything distracting in the background, you can also choose the option to stop the video for the participant.

There are other cool features like the one for Spotlight to keep someone on the screen while others are talking, you can make someone else a co-host and give them more permissions, you can allow people to record and you can also remove someone.

Share the Screen

The share screen being one of the most important features of Zoom allows the host to share the screen with his participants. The share screen gives the host the ability to allow the participants to see what he wants to present to them.

The share screen allows for interactive talk, sharing of files, working through a document together, giving a web tour, and also for holding tutorials or any other educational activities. An illustration can be given with the use of screen sharing through the whiteboard. Before you start screen sharing on Zoom, you should open all programs or windows you intend to share.

Share Screen Toolbars

These are the tools used in carrying out some tasks in the shared screen feature

Let's quickly discuss the toolbars above

Unmute/ Mute: This allows you to mute your microphone so that the participants can hear you and also unmute your microphone if you want them to hear from you.

Start video: With this, the host can decide to stop or start the video

Manage Participants: This allows you to manage participants such as mute/unmute microphones, start/stop the camera, lock screen, share, lock the meeting, etc.

New Share: This allows you to go back to the screen selection window to share a different window and restart a window that has been shared before.

Pause/Share: This allows you to pause a window being shared and also to continue it after being paused

Annotate: This is used to make online drawing, text insertion within the screen sharing in the Zoom window. It is also used to point out important information with a spotlight tool.

More: This tool opens a drop-down menu that contains additional menu items like chat, breakout room, invite, record to the cloud, disable attendee annotation

Now let's talk on how to share screen on a Zoom application.

How to Share Screen

Let's assume you host a meeting you intend sharing a file that requires you to share the screen, this is how to go about it

STEP - 01

Click on the share screen button below the screen

STEP - 02

Here in this place, some windows will pop up showing you what you can share, click on what you intend sharing

STEP - 03

What you click will be seen in this page

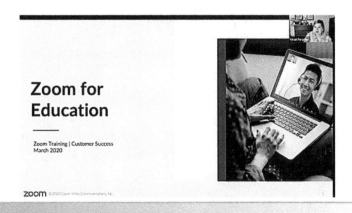

Create A Waiting Room

The easiest way to eliminate intruders is in the waiting room. With the waiting room, attendees cannot join the meeting until the host individually permits them from the waiting room. If the waiting room feature is enabled, the option for the invitees to join the meeting is disabled until the host arrives.

In the waiting room, the host can check if there is an intruder among the invitees, and if there is, he removes the intruder.

Let's quickly talk about how to enable the waiting room

STEP - 01

When you open your Zoom application, go to your settings

STEP - 02

Move to the hand right side and scroll down to the waiting room and turn on the waiting room

STEP - 03

When the meeting commences, the host can see the invitees at the right-hand side before he admits or remove them

CHAPTER - 4

Starting Your Class in Zoom by Starting a Meeting

To start a meeting, just log on to the web and click on "Host a Meeting." There you can choose whether you want to turn on the webcam or just share the screen. Whatever you choose, then you'll be able to change it, so don't worry.

If you want to schedule a meeting for another time, go to Meetings > Schedule a New Meeting.

Create a meeting in Zoom

- Topic: The title of the meeting

- Description: If you want, put a description on it. I don't put it on.

- When: configure the date and period of the meeting.

- Duration: It is indicative. Very useful if you use the account with several people.

- Time zone: It is important to set it well so

that the participants know what time it is for them if they are in a different time zone. Also, if you integrate it with a dating management app like Calendly, it's even more important that it's okay.

- Registration: If you mark it as mandatory, each attendee will have to put their name and email before entering the room.

- Meeting ID: It is the identifying number of the meeting.

- Make a meeting in Zoom.

- Meeting password: the password to access it.

- Video: Set whether you want the host and participant video to be on or off when they enter the room.

- Audio: So that the audio comes through the phone or the computer. I recommend that you leave it in both, so that each one can choose.

Meeting options: Here are 5 options to consider:

- Enter before the host: The meeting starts before you arrive. Not recommended for security reasons.

- Mute participants when entering: So that the participants have the microphone deactivated when entering the meeting.

- Enable waiting room: Each participant needs your approval to enter the meeting. Only authenticated users can join: (registered and logged in)

- Record the meeting automatically: The meeting starts recording as soon as it starts.

- Alternate Hosts - To set other meeting hosts.

These are the options when setting up a meeting. You can also start a meeting from the desktop app.

Invite to a Meeting in Zoom

There are two options for inviting people to a Zoom meeting: before and during the meeting.

The most common is to copy the link that is generated just after creating the meeting and share it with the other participants, either by email, WhatsApp or any other means.

The second way is to start the meeting, click on the "Participants" button located in the lower bar and, in the window that opens on the right, press the "Invite" button

Meeting Interface and Options

Meeting Interface on PC

Gallery view: This is the viewing mode in which you see all meeting participants. The screen is divided into a maximum of 49 (7 x 7) frames in which each person is seen if the webcam is on. If not, you will see a gray box with your name.

Speaker view: While on this mode you only view the speaker or the speaker screen if he has enabled the "screen sharing" function. At the top, you will see some participants in quite small boxes. You can pass them by if they don't all fit on the screen.

Microphone: Used to turn the audio on and off, as well as to choose the microphone you want to use and configure it to your liking.

Video: It is used to turn the video on and off, to choose the webcam you prefer and to set all the settings you want, such as the virtual background.

Security: This option comes to reinforce the security of your meetings with such interesting options as "Lock meeting" or "Enable waiting room."

Meeting Options in Zoom

Participants: You can see who are present in the class / meeting and whether the audio and video are activated or not. If you're a host, you can turn them on or off as you wish.

Chat: The feature allows you to access the chat to connect via the text with the other participants.

Screen Sharing: This is where you can share the screen of your device. The possibility of activating a virtual whiteboard with which to reinforce your explanations is also included.

Record: Activating this button, you can record the session. User can choose to pause and resume it each time they want. You can also stop it entirely.

Reactions: A new tab that appears when the host activates the camera. Let's clap and give the OK (thumb up smiley).

End meeting: You can end the meeting here if you're the host. If not, it will put "Exit the Meeting", option that you can also select as host.

The Zoom interface is further simplified if you click on "Switch to full screen." The advantage is that you focus more on the speaker, its screen, or other users; the disadvantage, that the other functions (chat, participants) open in a pop-up window and not on the side.

In the smartphone app, the interface is easier.

CHAPTER - 5

How to Present Yourself in Video Chat with Your Students

Even though we all know that you are likely to be at home when participating in a zoom 'class', it's still important to note that one should try to look presentable especially because you'll be facing your students. So, I'm going to share my top tips and tricks for looking your best in zoom 'classes'.

Use the Most Suitable Lighting

The best lighting is going to be the diffused natural light from a window that you're sitting directly in front. Any light that's coming from above you or from the side or from the back is not going to be that flattering because it's going to cast shadows or it's going to backlight you. However, if you're going to sit by a window, make sure that you're not going to sit in front of a window that gives you full exposure to direct sunlight because the lighting will just be too bright and it will blast you out.

Before a video zoom 'class', try to find out the area of the room or house that has the best lighting angle so you won't be embarrassed trying to adjust your position when the class starts. You can do this by using your phone camera to walk around the house or room to get the best angle.

To further enhance the lighting of your video, you can bring the bed lamp close to you or even put just opposite your face so that the light is shining directly on your face. You can also get a ring light if you can get access to it.

Use Your Most Suitable Camera Angle

Just like we were looking for the most flattering light, you've also got to be looking for the most flattering camera angle. I found out that the worst camera angle is always from below your face, anything from below your face will show all of your chin. You'll be looking down and the camera will be focusing on your chin, probably focusing on your neck wrinkles.

To get the best angle, look slightly up into the camera. That makes you lift your chin up slightly and it also helps to keep your eyes a little bit more open. To get your computer to your eye level or slightly higher, have your laptop set up on top of a small box or a thick book. You don't want it to be so high up that you can't reach it. Just adjust it finely till it looks just fine.

Avoid Touching Your Phone

Yes, don't touch your phone. Handling your phone when an important class is going on kind of won't speak well of you, so keep your phone away unless it necessary then. To keep your hands occupied, keep maybe a fine mug in front of you and keep your hand on it if you can't do without touching anything.

Put a Little Effort into Your Hair and Your Makeup

I'm not saying you have to go full-on glam and put on a full face of makeup and curl your hair but where people are going to be basically seeing only the torso part of you, you would try to make that part of you look a little bit better. But you shouldn't make yourself look like someone unrecognizable.

Just put on a little bit of mascara or possibly a neutral lipstick, it can make a big difference or maybe just a little lip balm.

Also put in the bare effort to tidy up and tie your hair or brush it well for the guys. Just do whatever you need to do to make yourself look a little bit more presentable, you don't want to go on camera looking dirty.

Keep the Distractions to a Minimum and Keep Your Background Neat and Tidy

This is just basic logic and common sense. Your environment must be neat and tidy. If you'll you be doing lots of zoom video classes, then it's advisable to make your study permanently setup for video classes.

It always has to be neat so you can sit down any time of day or night, if you get called into a meeting suddenly you don't want to be scrambling to clean up your filming space. Keep your space nice and neat.

Another distraction is when people are staring at themselves in the monitor instead of looking at the people that they're supposed to be talking to you. In a zoom video class, there are like five or twenty little images on the screen and you can see everyone. It's advisable to look directly at the person you are talking to instead of just staring blanking at the computer. Keep the distractions of playing with your hair, touching your face, pitching your nose, sticking your finger in your ear to a minimum. No one wants to see that; it can be annoying and gross.

Another distraction that you have to minimize are noise distractions from your family and your pets.

Dress Appropriately for Your Class

Everyone knows that everyone else is working from home but you definitely shouldn't be wearing like an oversized hoodie or something like that, and since you're only filming from the torso up whatever you're wearing on the top doesn't have to match what you have going on at the bottom.

You can still have your nighties or your sweats or whatever you want waist down. Just make sure that if you're going wear your nighties waist down, make sure that you have all your things for the class assembled in front of you so that you won't have to get up to get something and expose that you're actually not quite dressed well. It might be embarrassing to you and rude to others in the class.

CHAPTER - 6

Free Zoom vs Paid Zoom

The platform offers 4 types of subscription plans based on the number of participants, duration of the meeting, and the amount of cloud storage that is offered.

1. Zoom Free (Level 1): As the name suggests, you can access this plan for free. This level can host up to 100 participants at a time and conduct a meeting that can last up to 40 minutes. But you cannot record the

meetings.

2. Zoom Pro (Level 2): This level lets you create personal meeting IDs, record the meetings in your device's cloud, and conduct meetings up to 24 hours. You, as a host, will be charged $14.99 per month.

3. Zoom Business (Level 3): Apart from the basic features, Zoom Business lets you host meetings using your company's branding and specific URLs. Also, you can access the transcripts of the recordings in the cloud. What's more? You are eligible for customer support. You, as a host, will be charged $19.99 per month for Zoom Business.

4. Zoom Enterprise (Level 4): This plan is ideal for companies that have more than 1,000 employees. You get unlimited cloud storage and special discounts on webinars. You are also eligible for a discount on Zoom Room. A customer success manager is dedicated to your service. You, as a host, will be charged $19.99 per month for Zoom Business.

Setups

Now, there are two types of setup available on this platform: Zoom Meeting and Zoom Room. The former is focused on meetings that are held on this platform, and the latter is a hardware setup that is used for scheduling these Zoom

Meetings. You need an another subscription to access Zoom Room.

Zoom Meeting

As the name suggests, Zoom Meeting is a setup that hosts multiple users at the same time and allows seamless video conferencing to conduct important meetings or to host informal virtual gatherings. Even if you don't have a Zoom account, you can access this platform to join a Zoom Meeting. These meetings are attainable through devices such as laptops and phones, and a webcam or a video conferencing camera.

Zoom Room

As explained, Zoom Room is accessible from conference rooms and can help in scheduling Zoom Meetings and virtual discussions. Basically, this hardware system used to run Zoom Meetings is driven by dedicated software that is extremely simple to use. With a touch of a button, you can schedule, launch, and run a Zoom Meeting. This setup is beneficial for companies with large teams that need frequent discussions.

This service offers you a 30-day trial before buying the full subscription of Zoom Room. It lets you determine its efficiency and utility before you make a purchase decision. To buy this plan, you'll be paying $49 per month.

For a Zoom Room setup, you need the following tools:

- A computer or laptop to sync, launch, and run Zoom Meetings

- A microphone, a speaker, and video conference camera

- 1 or 2 HDTV monitors to screen-share important presentations and display participants

- An HDMI cable to connect the TV monitors and computer screens

- An internet cable and a stable internet connection, or reliable Wi-Fi

- A tablet for participants to launch and run the Zoom Meetings

CHAPTER - 7

How to Use Zoom to Teach Math

I f you're thinking how else you can expand the experience of learning Math or using Zoom your Math classes, here are some creative ways to employ.

Problem of the Week

Aptly known as POW, a Problem-of-the-Week can be anything that you feel needs more attention. It can be a problem you have identified, or a problem that your students can identify. You can create games that can help students learn about the problem differently.

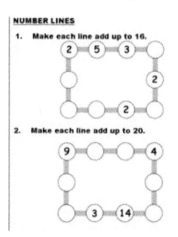

Link Interactive Simulations

There are several websites dedicated to providing helpful Math simulations. Sites like Explore Learning have thousands of Math simulations and variations that students can look up to solve mathematical problems. You can link these URLs in Zoom Chat, either as part of an assignment or through an announcement.

Use Whiteboard

Zoom's Touch Whiteboard will be discussed more in detail in the next chapter.

Use Digital Tools

Digital tools can also be used to solve various math problems. These tools can be used from Google Drive and integrated with Google Docs.

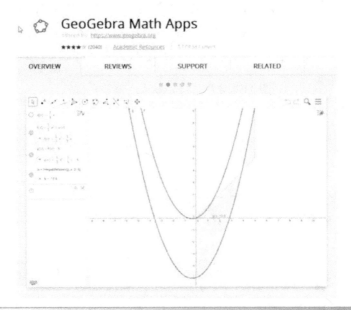

Other Teaching Methods to Use

Attach Patterns and Structures

Upload patterns and structures that students can identify and explain. Students can also collaborate with other student to identify patterns and structures to come up with solutions.

Use Geometric Concepts

Use Slides to insert drawings of geometric figures for Math, Science and even for Art.

Collaborate Online with Other Teachers

If you know other teachers have modules or projects which would come in handy with your class, collaborate and enable your students to join is as well. Different teachers allow for different resources and the teaching load can also be distributed.

Peer Tutoring

Senior students can also be allowed to access your Zoom Class at an agreed time on a weekly basis, to tutor and give support to junior students or students in differentiated assignments.

Celebrate Success

The teacher to encourage students through comments whenever they submit an assignment, because feedback can be given at once, and this can be done either private or publicly

Digital Quizzes

Quizzes can be used for various subjects. Get your students to submit their answers quickly for extra points.

Share Presentations

Share whatever presentations and slides that you have with your students to help them with assignments that you have given them.

Children are filled with natural curiosity. Somewhere during the formal process of schooling this wonder starts to disappear. It is as if the process of formal education replaces exploration and discovery with standardization, rules, and rigidity. Playing board games, puzzles and outdoor play also develop this type of thinking. Abstract thought is used by children when conceptualizing and understanding mathematics, though this type of thought begins with play (Seefeldt et al., 2012). According to Seefeldt et al., "Each of these types of play gives children practice in observing, sorting, ordering, comparing, counting, classifying, and predicting" (p. 8), all critical activities of mathematics. Providing opportunities for children to experience play at home (e.g., tiles in a kitchen, arranging toys) is an important part of developing abstract thinking that will ultimately strengthen students' mathematics learning.

To foster play at home think about the specific math skill you would want students to acquire and how you can contextualize this skill for play. For example, students can gather a collection of items to count so they practice counting and cardinality skills or create an array as an introduction to multiplication

Play can also be reinforced through digital games. Before we begin our work in 6th grade standards of equations students played the digital game SolveMe Mobile to build understanding of solving equations.

As a follow up to GamePlay, a project was introduced that would allow students to get creative while also developing an understanding 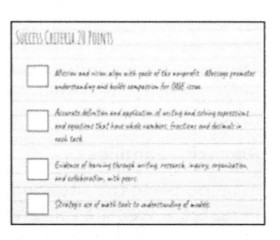 of procedures in solving equations. To further extend Math into the real world the students had to explore an issue they were concerned about and create a class non-profit. The project criteria and expectations were articulated in a slide deck so that students could work remotely.

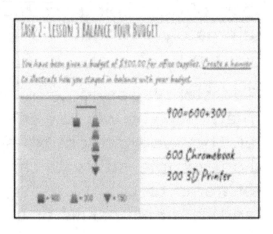

Students were given the choice of working collaboratively with a partner on this task. Elements of play were also included as students were tasked with using the SolveMe Mobile game to create a hanger that would represent a given situation. Play and projects can and should be intertwined to develop students' confidence and efficacy for doing the math. You might find that your most reluctant mathematicians become your most engaged when you include elements of play in tasks.

Play with Families

In response to the situation of remote teaching I created a website for families to include play at home. Play should include elements of interaction, collaboration, and critical thinking. Many of the Standards of Mathematical practice are visible when play is included in the math curriculum. Students must "Make sense of problems and persevere in solving them: whenever they take action in a game. Moreover, if they are playing with a partner there are greater opportunities to "Construct viable arguments and critique the reasoning of others" this happens quiet often when they need to explain their decision in a game. Games also provide an opportunity to "Look for and make use of structure" as the gameboard is fixed and provides a structure to which kids must look for patterns and see connections to become more efficient during game play.

Kids are natural gamers so don't feel the need to always create the game for play to happen. Upper elementary and secondary students can create their own Kahoot to share with their classmates. By providing an opportunity to create a game for play students are reinforcing skills and going deeper than their learning. There is nothing more high stakes than showing your work to your peers.

CHAPTER - 8

How to Use the Whiteboard in Zoom

Zoom Touch Whiteboard screen is an amazing feature for presentations/ teaching that you can quickly scribble something on, and you can also start drawing things and annotate on. You can explain things on it. It also has tools area where you can select text, drawing tool, spotlight eraser, etc., there are many tools there that you can use on your whiteboard for your presentations.

Using the whiteboard within a zoom meeting is incredibly useful but there were a couple of things that we need to be aware of and a couple of settings you need to be aware of so everything can run smoothly.

How to Use A Whiteboard

- Log into Zoom

- Join a meeting

- Tap meeting settings

- Tap on the Share Screen button

- Tap Whiteboard

- Tap Share

- The drawing/writing tools will come up automatically, but you can hide or show them.

- Use the drawing/writing (annotation) tools to making drawings, sketches or rough work on the whiteboard.

- You can save the whiteboard after the session as a PNG file. You can find it saved in your computer in Zoom folders as whiteboard. png.

- You can still use the whiteboard file for future references or send to people to work with.

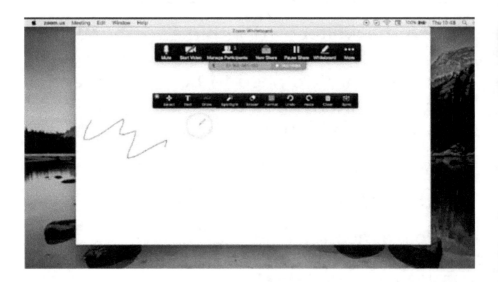

Whiteboard Drawing Methods

There are two types of drawing methods you can use to annotate on the whiteboard after starting a session in a zoom meeting for Touch. They are:

Free Form: This is just like freehand sketching. Zoom won't smooth out the sketches or convert the drawings to shapes. They will just remain as you drew them.

Smart recognition drawing: In this mode, zoom will smoothen out your lines and convert your drawings to shapes automatically after you sketch them on the touchscreen monitor.

These drawing methods are also available when annotating on a participant's shared screen.

Sharing Whiteboard in Desktop

- Log in to Zoom.

- Click the Whiteboard and tap on Share Screen.

- As you tap on the Whiteboard, the annotation tools will be available.

- You can also save the whiteboard as a Jpeg or Png file in your computer. It will be stored in the folder for zoom.

- You can create and switch between pages using the page controls in the bottom-right side.

- To stop, just tap on Stop Share.

Sharing Whiteboard In iPhone

- Log in to Zoom

- Host a meeting

- Click Share Content in the meeting settings, it's at the top-right side of the screen.

- Click on Whiteboard.

- The annotations tools will appear by default though you can click the pen tool to hide and show them.

- Click Stop Share when you are done.

Sharing Whiteboard in Android Phone

- Log in to Zoom

- Host a meeting

- Click Share Content in the meeting settings,

it's at the top-right side of the screen.

- Click on Whiteboard.

- Click the pen tool icon to show the annotation tools.

- Click the pen tool icon to hide the annotation.

- Click Stop Share when you're done.

There are two functions here that are very specific to this whiteboard.

1. You can enable and disable the participants annotations.

2. You can also show the names of the annotators. You will see that all their names will show up on your screen as they are making their annotations.

This is incredibly useful if you're doing a collaborative project and you do want them to annotate and add their own information to your whiteboard.

CHAPTER - 9

How to Make Students Understand that a Lesson on Zoom is Like a Real Classroom Lesson

Communication is very crucial in online teaching. Speaking in an effective manner is one of the problems that online tutors face. Often, we create a beautiful course that is captivating and attractive, but teaching the course is a big issue.

In this chapter, I will explain the various strategies that you can use to communicate with your students. Applying these tricks will help you to win the heart of your students quickly. If you are already an online tutor, you can also apply these tricks in your online teaching. Let's look at them one after the other.

Communicate Respectfully

Take note of this when communicating with your students. Respect is the pillar for every effective communication, especially when it has to do with students. While sitting on the computer, it is easier to forget that there are students on the other side. Sometimes, students might ask you provoking questions. You might be pushed to reply to the student in a thought-provoking manner. But it is wrong. Always pause and meditate before you lash out to the student. Avoid character attacks or unnecessary accusations. If you disagree with your student on issues. Look for a way to address what they are saying rather than attacking them.

While teaching, most notably during live videos, you'll encounter a situation where the student isn't paying attention. Sometimes, you encounter a situation where the student will ask you questions that you have answered repeatedly. It is on you, to calm down and address the situation. Like I said earlier, think about it that you are teaching your students offline. It will help you handle some issues.

Below is a summary of ways you can prove respectful communication.

Make use of a tone that is courteous and honest: That is, choose words that are appropriate to the situation. Avoid using inflammatory words. That is words that can infuriate the students or cause an emotional response.

Focus on what you are teaching: Avoid things that can distract you when you're teaching your students online. Sometimes, you see teachers walking out of the camera to attend to some needs and returning later. Most of those actions can infuriate the students. So, once you walk into your camera, focus on what you want to teach.

Apologize for your mistakes: Learn to apologize when you make a mistake. Some emergency might come up, and you will have to end the class abruptly. Apologize for ending the class and give the students tangible reasons while you need to end the class. It is very disrespectful, ending a live class without giving reasons.

Use clear and concise words

When you're communicating with your students, be clear as much as possible. It will help your students to understand you very well. Before you say something, give thought to what you want to say. Think about how your students will respond to such questions. Don't confuse your students with unclear sentences. If the topic is tough, look for a way to divide it into parts. In that way, your students won't struggle to understand it. Remember that they will only continue to enroll in a course that they are understanding. If your students do not understand what you're teaching, most of them will quit. Be brief when you are teaching. Avoid unnecessary words that are irrelevant. Sometimes, I see courses that are filled with stories that don't relate to the course. Try and make your session to be brief and straight to the point.

Make your communication personal

What do I mean? What I mean is making your communication feel real with the students. Make your students feel your presence. Communicate with your students in a way that they know you feel that they are real people and that you respect and value your communication with them.

An effective way to do that is by having a class discussion from time to time. In the class discussion, every student will be availed of the opportunity to interact with each other. It will boost the confidence of the students.

Start and End with Key points

In other words, to ensure that your students will understand your lesson, reiterate critical points at the start and end of the course. Another way to do that is by adding a footnote at the end of the course. The note will serve as a reminder to the students.

Connecting with Your Students

Having talked about the various ways that you can communicate with your students; it is also necessary that you learn how to connect with your students very well. The first step in doing this is by seeing yourself as a student. Picture yourself as your student. Ask yourself, "Why do I like this teacher?

So, for you to connect with your students very well, your students must love you and find your course appealing. It will be difficult to connect with someone that doesn't like your course. There are effective ways that you can connect with your students. The best way to connect with your students is to.

Appreciate your Students

You might not like it because you see it as degrading yourself. That's wrong. This tip works like magic. Always appreciate your students. Tell them how happy you are seeing them online. Try to recognize their presence. Whether you are doing prerecording or live video, always appreciate your students. If you know their names, you can mention them one by one. When you appreciate your students, they will love you more. They will feel comfortable sharing their problems with you.

Motivate your students

It is another factor that most tutors overlook when teaching online. But it is a crucial factor that you need to put into practice. You're teaching a distant student that you don't know the life experiences of. Most students study harder when someone inspires them. Be a motivator to your students. When you're teaching, use the avenue to motivate your students.

Listen

Listen to your student's problems, ideas, or contributions. What you are doing is teaching some set of people online. You aren't teaching ghosts. So, allow them to ask their questions, and you reply to them. Giving your students a listening ear will help them to understand your course quickly.

Create an Online community

It is another way to connect with your students. Most tutors add forums on their website where the students will communicate, crack jokes with one another. Creating a community will ease the pressures that the students are facing in a course. Your online community will also allow the students to share ideas, a solution to questions.

Give assignment that enables Students to Share their Experiences

Giving students a task that allows them to share their experience will also help you to connect with your students. The assignments can be essay writing, history projects, or anything – depending on your course.

CHAPTER - 10

How to Be an Innovative Teacher on Zoom

Creating student independence and responsibility regarding their own learning is by all accounts perhaps the best thing you can do to prepare your students for autonomy. Student autonomy, in any case, should be understood as a process instead of a state. It is frequently mistaken for empowering self-guidance, and this could absolutely be one of the results, yet the concept goes beyond that: By assuming responsibility for their learning, your students will turn out to be able to engage better in the class, try out more difficult projects, and learn better. In addition, it should help with boosting their innate motivation as they find their own voice.

So how can you empower student autonomy in your online classes?

1. Expand upon the students' earlier information.

2. Pick engaging settings and points.

3. Develop flexible tasks and tests.

4. Keep it dynamic.

5. Encourage cooperation.

6. Urge students to face challenges.

7. Give your students choices.

8. Get students to put in thought and contribute to their learning process.

9. Clarify why you do what you do.

Models

Here is a veritable model of student autonomy:

An autonomous student will set their own objectives, think about their growth, and look for chances to practice outside the classroom.

In the online classroom

Asking that students keep journals to think about and process the way in which they learn best, and showing them how to use tools, for example, word references can empower autonomy. Asking yourself if your students can do this by themselves? Ask yourself about any plans for class that can help create the right conditions for the advancement of greater student autonomy in class.

Principles

When it comes to the principles of creating autonomy, there are essential dos and don'ts.

Do's:

- Begin new learning assignments with opportunities for your students to ask questions and receive support and clarification from you or from fellow classmates if they are experiencing issues with understanding the ideas or work expected of them.

- Give your students important choices in line with the learning goals and activities. This will enable them to assess their knowledge of the subject matter and track their learning progress.

- Help your students handle the inescapable frustration that comes when they fail to perform as well as they thought they would, or if the learning process isn't going as smoothly as they expected it would go. For instance, you can teach your students how to use mistakes and failures as learning opportunities and how to control the negative emotions that can affect their ability to learn.

- Praise students for excelling on their assignments and for investing additional effort. Use clear praises that specifically tell your students what they are have improve on, what they are excelling at and what learning process or skill they are being praised for.

- Involve your students in setting goals and making decisions about how to personalize the goals following the educational program's requirements, in addition to individual and collective student interests and choices.

- Appeal to your students' interest by introducing them to new knowledge using the previous knowledge they have.

Don'ts:

- Link learning successes or failures to students' lack of capacities or insight. Students cannot change some of their learning abilities, but they can change learning habits and practices like effort and consistency.

- Compare individuals or groups of students with one another based on how fast or well they learn new material.

- Engage in teaching systems that allow students to be latent. Rather, connect with their interest and promote active learning.

- Ask your students to duplicate your learning methodologies. Rather, try to expand their attention to themselves as self-managed and vital students.

- Break down information without showing your students how the sections connect with the rest of the course, or the "big picture." Presenting detached realities without relating them back to the general subject or idea being taught makes it easy for your students to lose interest in the course.

- Provide students with choices without also helping them become more mindful of their own needs, interests, inclinations, weaknesses, strengths, goals, and expectations.

Small Teaching Online Quick Tip: Creating Autonomy

Here are some ways to create autonomy particularly through online discussions.

1. Request That Your Students Help Shape Conversation Necessities:

Your prospectus should show the significance of conversations in your online course and the learning goals they line up with. You could ask your students to offer feedback on this part of the learning plan and allow them to contribute to what class conversations look like and what the prerequisites will be.

2. Offer Choice in Conversation Prompts:

Students are bound to dive deeper into their work (and find importance in it) when they are looking for the questions that interest them, instead of the ones you have set for them. Another approach to promote student autonomy through your online conversations is to give your students different prompts to explore and ask that they react to one. Along these lines, your students would not feel compelled to discuss something they aren't interested in, and they can recognize the material and thoughts that interest them most.

3. Let Your Students Pick How to Answer:

Move away from standard written answers and permit your students to take part in conversations by recording voice answers, video answers, or short audiovisual presentations.

4. Give Your Students a Choice Between Simultaneous and Off-and-On Conversations:

While your simultaneous class groups probably won't be obligatory for online students, you could consider giving your students a choice between answering to conversations non-concurrently and participating in a coordinated web conferencing meeting (e.g., Zoom). This is an incredible method to consider students who like the spontaneity and natural eye-to-eye conversation. You could also record the meeting and afterward share it with the rest of the class, so nobody is left out of the learning opportunities these meetings give.

5.   Offer Alternative Options for Online Conversations:

Confer with your students and find out if they are interested in elective techniques for connection. This could include something like teaming up on comments using a tool like Hypothesis or making a Google Doc of shared notes.

Being open to student contribution to how online conversations are driven will help you with promoting student autonomy while urging students to connect with the course material and their classmates in important ways. By giving your students more choices with regards to online conversations, you can move past the tedious "I agree" to more thoughtful and deliberate conversations.

CHAPTER - 11

How to Get the Students' Concentration Throughout the Lesson

Even when teaching online, it is essential to create a classroom environment with which students want to interact. Live lesson sessions using technology can help create a classroom environment. Using excellent visual aids can help students find fun and joy in their learning. As a teacher, you can even use technology to record fun videos or organize live lesson sessions or individual conversations so students can interact with you in real-time. Students want and need such interaction with a teacher so that they can trust and learn well from them.

A narrative approach to teaching will help you create a classroom environment that keeps students engaged. Talk about yourself, tell stories, and create fun learning opportunities for students while being online. Call students by their names, remember some details about them, and create stories during the different lessons to create a fun and comfortable classroom environment. Online teaching is becoming increasingly popular today, and teachers are expected to go beyond their comfort zone to reach students. Technology is extremely helpful in helping teachers create meaningful learning environments within an online session.

Smart Ways to Engage Your Online Students

You as a teacher should be able to predict and address these problems by implementing the following strategies for keeping students engaged.

Regularly Update the Course Content

Why not do some research and development on various current affairs that might be of interest. The Internet is full of resources or lesson plans based on the latest developments. There are many online sources of information such as news websites, articles, videos, podcasts and conference session recordings. As a course designer, you could also incorporate recent policies, regulations or various reviews.

Whatever you choose as course content, it is always a great idea to take into account all the latest trends as well as emerging practices from various sectors.

Assign Successful Coaches

At many colleges and universities, successful coaches are assigned to students who attend online courses. These individuals provide tips on learning and studying online, as well as offer assets to aid students in dealing with tasks and managing time. A learning coach (you could call them what you want to) also helps students identify or plan their learning path, by directing students to external or resources.

The added value of successful coaches is significant since they take the online learning program to the next level. Coaches can also help students reach specific course milestones and avert any sidetracking or distractions.

Encourage Responsibility

There are some easy tweaks that you can do to follow up on students. Should you not have a Learning Management System (LMS), there is no need to worry. There are a number of tools, such as Remind, which allow instant yet safe communication among educators, parents and teachers.

The key point is to show students that they are not alone and are not neglected throughout this learning process. Such tools also allow for relaying comments or any kind of communication.

CHAPTER - 12

How Not to Get Cheated During the Tests

In online environments, there is the added perception of increased cheating (although this has been proven to be a myth - students can cheat just as easily in a face-to-face classroom). To address this, teachers often must institute very specific policies designed to ensure the academic integrity of their students.

Changing our thinking about the way we assess students is perhaps one of the greatest challenges we face as we make the transition to online environments. The good news is that this change does not have to happen overnight. There are both simple and complex ways to adapt assessments in online teaching and learning.

The multiple-choice can be quite useful in assessing short-term learning outcomes throughout the learning process and provides a quick way to gauge student understanding.

So, it is important to be aware of the right assessment strategies and the potential advantages and disadvantages associated with using them. Of course, in an era of standardized testing, it is impossible to remove yourself completely from the use of traditional objective tests.

As is true of many facets of teaching, being well prepared can reduce the likelihood that something will go wrong and thus alleviate your anxiety about it. To reduce students' potential for cheating, you should be aware of how students cheat:

- By allowing another person to take a test

- By looking at materials or searching for answers online

- By purchasing or copying materials from the Internet

- By finding the answers before taking the assessment or sharing answers with each other

New technologies for tracking and identifying test takers are in the early stages of development. For example, keyboard profile software, which creates an identifiable profile of keyboard strokes for an individual using a computer, may eventually make it to the mainstream. Webcams are an existing technology that can be used to identify or view the user as he or she takes a test. Other more conventional ways to remove the temptation to cheat include the following:

- Lower the stakes on multiple-choice tests or eliminate them entirely.

- Use alternate assessments and make the assessment part of the learning process.

- Personalize assignments.

- Incorporate assessments into live conferences.

- Use open-book and timed tests.

- Limit access to test questions, so that students see them one time and cannot backtrack.

- Randomize questions from a test bank.

- Proctor high-stakes tests.

When it comes to mandated school and state high-stakes testing, you should expect some differences in the process used online from that used in brick-and-mortar schools. In online programs, test administration may be handled throughout a region or state and often requires travel by teachers and others to test proctoring sites. Tests may be proctored in any number of places: universities, libraries, schools, and conference rooms.

Given the concerns expressed earlier and the significant lack of direct observation when students are being assessed, what are the accepted and appropriate assessment strategies in online environments? Can we borrow preferred strategies from traditional classrooms or higher education and apply them to K–12 online classrooms? If so, how?

Assessment Instruments

Before learning about specific strategies, you should become familiar with the types of instruments at your disposal for evaluating student learning. The most common assessment instruments include the following:

- Tests and quizzes: These objective assessment tools are useful for assessing students' factual knowledge. In addition, well-designed objective assessments can be effective at measuring higher-order thinking and conceptual understanding. They can be used both during instruction and at the conclusion of instruction. However, research has indicated that quizzes embedded in learning activities have not been effective in improving student outcomes (U.S. Department of Education, 2009).

- Self-evaluation: Learners reflect on their

individual learning to evaluate both the process and the product.

- Checklists: Simple checklists are useful for documenting participation and task completion throughout the learning process. They can provide measurable demonstration of student progress through identified milestones and goals.

- Rubrics: Rubrics are powerful tools for both informing learners about your expectations and for evaluating their learning. Rubrics can be especially effective in online environments for reinforcing written instructions.

- Surveys: The use of simple surveys and polls allows students to comment on the learning process and yield valuable feedback about the effectiveness of your instruction.

- Learning logs: A learning log provides a reflective, historical record of individual learning throughout the learning experience. Logs may or may not include artifacts.

- Portfolios: Portfolios are more structured than learning logs. They should incorporate evidence and artifacts demonstrating how students have met learning goals and objectives.

- Presentations: Delivering multimedia presentations provides an opportunity for students to demonstrate mastery of learning. Because of the wide range of free tools available, the format and delivery methods for presentations are virtually limitless. Consider books, guides, comics, drawings, animations and films in addition to the traditional slide-show presentation.

Assessment Tools

Many tools are available for assessing students online, and they have been perfected over time. Your LMS will contain tools for creating multiple-choice assessments with a host of options for limiting access, randomizing questions, self-scoring, requiring immediate response, and setting time limits. Options for summative and formative assessments might include fill-in-the-blank items for short-answer and essay exams and instructions to show work in math problems.

In addition, almost all LMSs have an automated grading process for assignment submissions, feedback, and discussion post ratings. And because student access to the LMS is tracked, most systems include valuable analytic tools and reports that can produce information to assess student engagement and participation. LMS reports can track where students have been, how often they have been there, and, in some cases, for how long. There are often multiple options for viewing whole-class or individual behavior—from information on a particular day and for a specific assignment to a range of dates, actions, and assignments. Once again, getting to know your LMS is of critical importance.

Process versus Product Assessments

Assessments can be examined from multiple perspectives. Formative and summative assessments are examples of common categories that define when assessments are used. Formative assessments can be conducted throughout the learning process; they are process oriented and designed to improve learning. Summative assessments are used at the end of the learning process; they are product oriented and designed to measure the amount of learning that has occurred. Both types of assessments are useful and have benefits and drawbacks.

Nonetheless, what may be more important than when assessments are used is how they are used. Categorizing assessments in terms of process (sometimes called performance-based assessments) and product comes closer to supplying a usable framework for evaluating their value. The table below further illustrates the differences in process and product assessments.

Types of process and product assessments and associated tools.

	Process	Product
Description	Formative Drives student learning Informal, procedural, and reflective	Summative Student work evaluated to determine what has been learned Formal and outcome based
Focus	Sequence of activities or tasks and performance improvement	Factual knowledge, conceptual knowledge, and mastery
Types	Assignments, artifacts, reflections, project participation, project contributions, and peer reviews	Multiple-choice exams, essays, short-answer responses, and expert evaluations
Instruments	• Self-evaluations • Self-reports • Checklists • Surveys • Activity logs • Communication tools • Learning logs • Collaborative writing tools • Live or archived meetings	• Rubrics • Quizzes • Tests • Portfolios • Learning logs • Presentations • Live or archived meetings • Portfolios • Discussion forums • Assignment submission tools
Example Tools	LMSs, wikis, blogs, RubiStar, and Web conference tools	LMSs, QuizStar, Quizizz, Kahoots, slide-sharing tools, and Web conference tools

Performance-Based Assessments

Performance-based assessments are process oriented. This means that the process of assessment should inform both the teacher and the learner about progress toward instructional goals and objectives. The process of assessment is just as important as—and may be more important than—the type of assessment used.

Part of the process includes the feedback loop. Feedback is essential to student learning and is probably more important in online environments because of the lack of immediacy. Instructors should take special care to ensure that feedback is timely, meaningful, and frequent. There are many opportunities to provide feedback in online environments, including feedback on assignments and on discussion forum posts and dialogue in collaborative activities. Embedded opportunities for feedback can also be provided through self-evaluation.

Whatever feedback options you choose, you should develop a clear and consistent plan that includes the following information:

- Where feedback is provided (e.g., email, LMS, or phone)

- How feedback is provided (e.g., written or oral; rubric or exam score; peer, self, or instructor)

- When feedback is provided (e.g., reasonable expectations for timely feedback)

CHAPTER - 13

Tips & Tricks

The Zoom platform is an excellent answer to video interaction and communication problems faced by businesses and large organizations. The platform comprises of several essential scale and attributes. It is, therefore, important to understand several tips and tricks of the program. Below are a few tricks that you should know to improve your experience:

Use virtual background

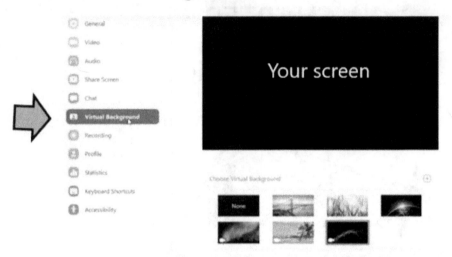

The platform consists of various attributes, but this is a wonderful one. It lets users attach a custom background to their project. It could be in the form of materials like an image or video during the interaction. It also yields several out of the box media, and users can include their video or picture to the background of their project.

The program can differentiate between the background and the face of the user in real-time. You must enable the feature if you want to use it. Select the Cogswell logo to launch settings and navigate to the virtual background. In this section, you can decide what type of image and navigate to the virtual background. You can choose several available options.

Enhanced Beauty

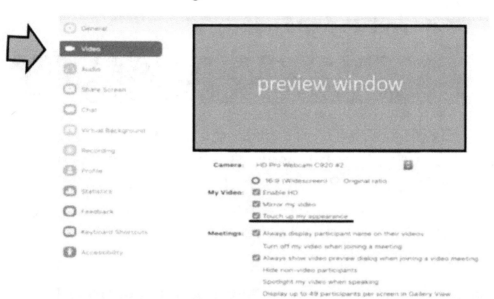

The platform can help users prepare for the intended meeting by beautifying them. It has an attribute with the name touch my appearance. It is a filter that adds smoothness to the surface of the skin. It isn't an aggressive filter and also make minimal modification to the face. You can hardly notice the difference. It keeps the natural look of the face, and you can set it up before participating in the video interaction. You can perform that task with a few clicks. Follow the steps below:

· Launch the app

· Select the gear logo beneath the picture of the account

· Tap video

- Tuck the touch my appearance box

Mute and un-mute mic

It is one of the most interesting attributes of the platform. It gives users the power to minimize and eradicate background noise and cross-talks, especially when there are lots of attendants on the video interaction. You can perform this task with a simple click.

For instance, if you find yourself in a conference on the web and have nothing to contribute at that moment, you can easily mute your mic and whenever you want to contribute, you can turn it back for usage. You can turn it on by holding your space bar, which will turn on the mic, and you can start talking. If you take your hands off the space bar, the mic goes mute again.

The feature ensures that you have a smooth interaction without interruptions and do not take lots of bandwidth. It also offers excellent clarity of voice, which means that everyone can hear each other. If you want to utilize this attribute, launch settings, select audio, allow mute mic anytime you want to join an interaction. It makes the whole process easy and straightforward.

Disallow Videos When You Want to Join a Video Interaction

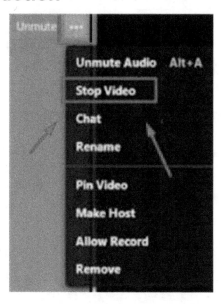

At some point in time, you might get a video alert and join the call quickly without preparation and the platform offers a solution to fix that problem. The disallow feature can save you from that embarrassment. There is an option for you to disallow the feature permanently anytime you want to link up with an interaction. Whenever you're fit enough to face the camera, you can turn it back on and use it. If you want to utilize this attribute, navigate to your settings and launch it, select the video and allow turn my video off anytime you join a meeting.

Allow Gallery View

There are several attributes that the platform includes, but you will love and admire this one.

It keeps everyone on one page, and you 'keep track of all the attendants in the interaction in one place at a time. You can also avail this attribute anytime you put together small groups, and you must turn it on if you want to use it. To allow it, select a gallery view, and you can enjoy the outstanding experience it offers.

Automatically Copy Invitation URL

If you want to invite lots of attendants to your video interaction, you must utilize a global attribute that the platform offers, which you can utilize to copy invitation URL and place it on your clipboard. You can save lots of time by selecting invite and locating the URL for it. So, launch settings and toggle general, then allow automatically copy URL anytime the interaction begins. You can start sending the invites to attendants that you want to participate by distributing the link to social media and several platforms with ease.

Utilize Snap Camera

It is the desktop category of snap chat that gives users the power to include several filters to beautify them from the application so that they can build lenses. Users can distribute the lenses with the platform and set it as a default. The attribute is a wonderful one that you'll enjoy using especially if you put together a group call to your relatives or friends.

If you want to use it, you need to get its app for the version of your device and select an image utilizing any of the available lenses. After performing that task, launch the app and navigate your way to settings. Beneath the section for video, modify the location of the camera from the menu that drops down to the snap camera feature.

Share Your Screen

It is one of the most outstanding attributes of the platform, and everyone can use this one. Lots of companies make use of this function for remote or online help, while few users share visuals to see a movie or watch together. You must turn the feature on if you want to use it.

To use it, just start a video interaction and select the share screen beneath the page. You can also allow the feature for the active window or the entire visual display. For maximum experience, you should turn on the device around.

Unify Third-Party Applications

The platform has lots of compatibility with third-party apps that you can unify easily with one tap. If you want to take part in meetings through the platform, get the app from the store, and you're good to go. You can also utilize the feature to import the schedules you create for the interaction through outlook or the calendar app from Google.

You can meet relatives and business partners on several platforms and begin interaction with only one click. You should know that you can find an app that can perform that function very well. You can find every app that you require on the platform store.

Allow Records

Another important trick that the platform can perform is recording conversation held by the entire group of people involved in the interaction. For example, you can record the interaction on your gadget by tapping the record control key while the interaction is in progress and it will begin.

The files of the conversation will be inside the documents section. The platform can also provide recordings via the cloud, but only users of a certain stage can utilize this feature; the paid accounts can enjoy this benefit.

Audio Transcript

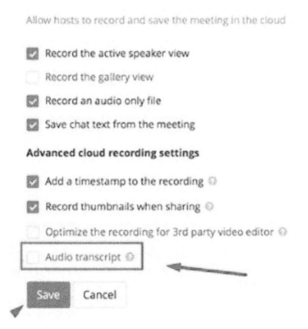

The platform consists of an important attribute that users can use to transcribe the audio recordings of an interaction automatically.

Users can use it to keep records and important parts of interaction inside a VTT text file. Only paid accounts that want to record via cloud have the opportunity to utilize this attribute.

If you are one of the paid accounts, you should launch the platform browser for recording and allow records for the cloud. Now select advanced settings and tick allow on the audio transcript. Anytime you find yourself in an interaction, select record for cloud beneath the page. The platform will send an email after a few minutes, notifying you of the status of the transcript.

Create a Schedule for Interactions

You will find the option to create an interaction schedule on the desktop app of the platform. You need to launch the app, and that can waste a little bit of your time. But if you wish to perform that task quickly, get the scheduler which is a free extension for you to use. Add an event there.

Stealth mode

It is a wonderful attribute associated with the platform. It ensures that users gain access to video interactions with no sound. It is wonderful to use when you get access when the interaction is in progress and want to avoid interruption at all cost. It is important to fix your device mic.

Launch the app and select settings.

Tick boxes you wish to include from the audio section to mute the mic anytime you enter an integration beneath the visual display.

You can participate in an interaction without turning your video on, which is important for low bandwidth areas and location with quality problems.

Launch the app and select settings.

Tick the turn video off anytime you want to take part in an interaction.

To toggle on the mic, tap the control key beneath the visual display while the conversation is on.

Emoji on Screen

If the host of an interaction mutes your account, you can display your reaction with the use of emoji. You can decide which to send, and there are lots of available options, including the clapping and thumbs up. It is easy to communicate your feelings with it.

Whenever you want to use in an interaction, select reactions beneath the visual conversation display, and select your desired choice. It can disappear in less than ten seconds. If the interaction admin allows the nonverbal response attribute, attendants can put a logo like raising a finger, which shows that they want to contribute to the interaction. Everyone in the group can see the emoji replies.

Accommodate Above One Hundred People

You can put together more than one hundred people together in one meeting, which is a wonderful advantage for schools and business organizations. But you need a paid account to enjoy that feature.

If you subscribe to the premium package, you can invite and accommodate at least one thousand attendants. It is also wonderful advantage for remote and online workers because they can use the platform to communicate with co-workers as well as relatives.

Zoom Paid Plans

The platform is free for everyone; you can even use it without signing up. Though, you should know that the platform comes with different plans. The basic plan gives access to a limited number of minutes for the interaction, which is forty minutes.

If you go for the pro plan, it supplies a twenty-four-hour limit, which you can consider a lot of time if that is what you require to complete your project. You can also use the platform to run your organization even if you do not have wireless.

The platform lets every user host video interactions with at least one hundred people multiple times. The Pro Plan offers at least one gigabyte of cloud storage for your recording activities, an increased time duration for the interaction, and improved add-ons. It is also an important feature for large companies because of the number of people it can accommodate.

Waiting Room

There have been reports about hackers and malicious people trying to Zoom bomb interactions without authorization, which makes it important to avail this attribute that the platform provides. It gives you the power to accommodate attendants one after the other or hold everyone in the waiting room.

To allow the attribute, launch the app settings on a browser and navigate to account management. Toggle on the attribute. You can now decide who should go to the room. It will stop intruders from interrupting your interactions. If you are unavailable to allow an attendant, you should enable internal attendants to identify attendants from the room. Select save, and that's all. Only premium accounts can enjoy this benefit.

Send a Quick Invitation

Whenever you are in an interaction, and you remembered that you didn't invite a particular person related to the topic of discussion. You can solve that problem quickly wit this attribute. Launch the invite page and select email, copy the address, and transfer it to the person to invite them into the conversation. You can perform this task with your workers as well as friends and family.

Breakout Room

If you want to have a large webinar or interaction, users can easily split it into various rooms with different sessions. The creator of the interaction can designate sub-hosts that can handle attendants in the rooms.

The platform gives you the power to build fifty breakout rooms that can accommodate two hundred attendants. If you create thirty rooms, it can accommodate four hundred attendants. You can allow this attribute from the platform web portal settings. Then find your way to the room option and toggle it on. You need to know that only paid users can enjoy this benefit.

CHAPTER - 14

Most Crucial Settings in Zoom

I would like to share with you some of the crucial settings to activate or deactivate in Zoom for you to make the most of the platform.

- Make sure that people can join by either telephone or computer audio by toggling on the

Telephone and Computer Audio option. Sometimes, the internet connection might not be good, but you can still talk on the telephone. This could also enable people to join the meeting, whether they are stuck in traffic, camping, or even at the Airport. Ensure you open up the possibilities for everyone to participate from wherever they are.

To activate your Telephone and Computer Audio feature, go to Settings> Audio Type>Telephone and Computer Audio.

STEP - 01

Ensure people can join before the host by toggling on the Join before the host option. This enables participants to join the meeting before you. To activate this setting go to Settings> Toggle on Join before host

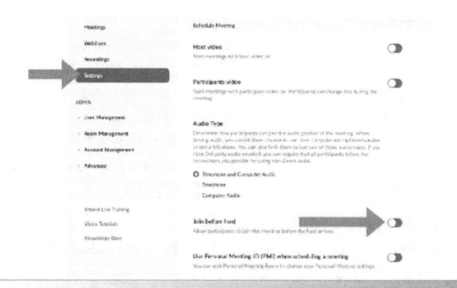

STEP - 02

You also have the option to play a sound when any of the participants join or leave the meeting. You can decide if you want the music to be Heard by the host and all participants or Heard by host only.

STEP - 03

Toggle on the Allow host to put attendee on hold option. This enables the host to remove an attendee from the meeting temporarily.

STEP - 04

It would be best if you toggled on the Always show meeting control bar. This will enable you to control the meeting better.

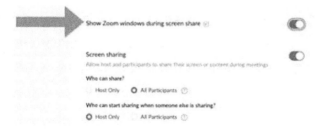

STEP - 05

When you toggle on Show Zoom windows during screen share option, it enables you to see the zoom participants during Screen share.

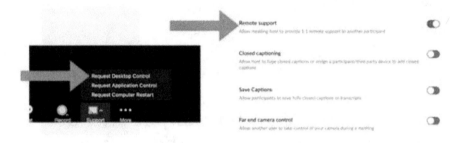

STEP - 06

If you toggle on Remote Support, you can access a participant's screen so that you can control or assist any of the participants.

Ensure you have your Zoom Waiting room set up. Turn on the waiting room, and in a paid account, you can personalize the waiting room such that you can add your logo or special message for people. In the free account, it just has a generic message "Please wait, the meeting host will let you in soon."

What it does is that it allows people to wait. You can let everybody go in at once, or you as the host can make people go in one at a time. This is a good way to staying in charge of your meetings.

STEP - 07

Toggle on Show a "Join from your browser" link. This ensures that people can join the meeting using a browser link. They can skip downloading the software while trying to join and view the meeting on their browser. Although they won't have as much interactive ability, if someone is on a chrome book, that doesn't have the space to download or install a new application or are on a public computer, they will have no better option but to join via a browser link.

Please wait, the meeting host will let you in soon.

Ben and Jade Balden's Personal Meeting Room

STEP - 08

Toggle on When attendees join meeting before host option. This will allow you to get notified via Email whenever a new person is entering a meeting. I have gotten this notification once or twice, where I have forgotten about an appointment, and then I got a notification Email that someone just joined the meeting. That immediately reminded me of the schedule.

Email Notification

When attendees join meeting before host.
Notify host when participants join the meeting before them

How to Set Up a New Meeting

Simply click on Schedule a meeting. You can name it what you want, and then it reminds you that if it is not a paid account that when you have three or more people, it will cut you off at forty minutes. You can adjust the settings for a meeting, and then hit Save when you are done.

One of the settings I like to use is to use one meeting ID. Even when I have several meetings I just give people one meeting ID link, and then I use that same link for all of my meetings, because I am now able to control who is going to be there or not.

In the paid version, you'll find at the bottom of the screen, the Poll icon. This also allows you to set up a poll. Polling during your meeting is one of the paid benefits.

- They are basic questions that you can put in your answers. You have single and multiple-choice questions.

When you have your meeting all set up, you need to go to Meeting and click on Copy Meeting Invitation. You will get something to copy and send to people via any social media platform you wish.

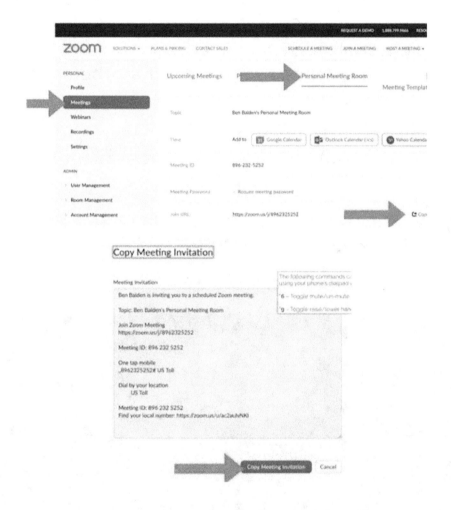

When you need to go and edit the meeting again, when you open up the meeting from your browser, click on Edit this Meeting. When you're done editing, click Save.

I find it helpful to play around the software both from your computer and phone to see how things look. It is beneficial to do that to ensure you're acquainted with everything before the meeting time.

One more thing to note is that in the paid version, you can also choose your meeting ID number.

You can use your phone number for this so that it can be easy to remember.

Now that we have it all set up let's dive into it!

Zoom Virtual Meeting Room

Think of your Zoom meeting room as a virtual meeting room where everybody will meet at the same time in the same location, so you need to get the word out there. The location is the link that you are going to send out to people.

The first step is to invite people to the Meeting. Remember that earlier; we looked at how to copy the meeting invitation.

When you copy the link, you can have your team send it as an email to people, or a text message, or any social media platform. The link on the invitation is the most important thing.

You can also invite once you've started the meeting by tapping on the Invite icon and then sending the link to participants. It is very easy to get people in.

Joining the Meeting

Once you have sent out the link, participants can join from almost any device. Though, there is a little difference between joining from a computer and a mobile device.

From a computer:

- You can join from a browser

- It is easy to share screen

- You can conduct polls

- You can record to computer

From a Mobile App

- You must download App

- Different UI

- You can't see the video and the chat at the same time.

To join the Meeting, you can either open up the App or the program on your computer or click on New Meeting or Join or Open New Meeting. You can do it from a browser. Go to Meeting> personal meeting room> start a meeting. That gets you into the meeting. For everybody else, you can give them a link. They can type it into their browser or click on the link to join the meeting directly.

Launching...

Please click Open zoom.us if you see the system dialog.

If nothing prompts from browser, click here to launch the meeting, or download & run Zoom.

If you cannot download or run the application, join from your browser.

If they do not have Zoom app installed on their computer, it would prompt them to install it. They can either click on the link to install it or join through their browser.

If people are joining from their browser, they should click on Join from your browser. It will ask them to input their name, before joining.

When you join the meeting, this is what it will look like before you turn on your video.

When someone else joins the meeting, you can admit them, if you have waiting room set up. If you do not have waiting room set up, it would just allow them join right in.

For those using a device, when they click on the link, it will prompt them to download the app. They can go ahead and download the app from their App store. Once they have gotten the app downloaded, they may need to click on the link again, because sometimes, it gets lost in the process. Next, it brings them to the start screen.

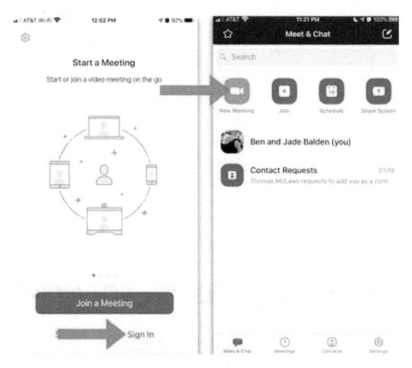

If they didn't click on the link, they can click on Sign in and input their meeting ID. If they are joining from a mobile device, they can click on New Meeting When you are in the meeting, and someone joins, if you have the waiting room set up, you can go ahead and admit them from there, or click on the waiting room. They will have all the functionalities that everyone else has. They can swipe left to right to talk. There is a driving mode where they can listen, and they click on a button to speak as well.

Navigating Zoom

Now that we have gotten everybody inside the meeting, let us talk about navigating around once you're in there.

There are two different views.

- Gallery View: This view enables you to see everybody's face.

- Speaker View: When someone is speaking, and their volume is louder than everybody else's. The app will think that they are the predominant speaker or presenter and then put a green halo around their screen.

If you're on a mobile device, it will just bring the speakers screen to the front.

If a participant has a background noise and is brought the front. You as the presenter can just mute them by first clicking on Manage Participants at the bottom of the screen and then hover over the person's name and then click Mute. You can mute and unmute everybody at the same time as you wish.

You can mute and unmute yourself just by clicking on the Mic icon. You can adjust your sound as well.

With Video, you can either turn on or turn it off, just by clicking on the video icon. You can also adjust your video settings from there.

Share Screen

This can be done on a mobile device or a computer. Although, a computer gives you a lot of options.

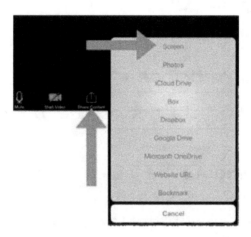

You can plug in a mobile device, or on a Mac computer, you can use airplay mode for your mobile device. It enables you to show people how to navigate through something on their phone during a meeting, which is super helpful. You can share your web browser. You can even share your entire screen.

On the app on your mobile device, you can click on Share screen, and then start a broadcast, which is a new feature.

You'll be notified that your participants will be able to see everything you have on your screen, including your notifications.

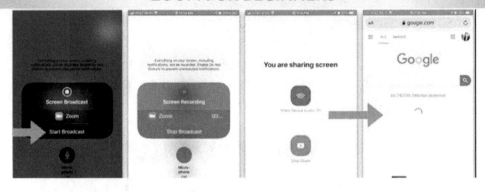

Managing Participants

Click on Participants at the bottom of the screen.

You're going to be able to see how many participants are present in the meeting. You can mute and unmute them, and you can see a little bit of the kind of interaction you're having with them.

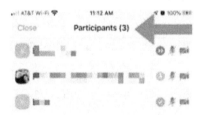

Chat

There is a way to enter the chat mode. And chat with everyone or chat with just with people individually.

Share Files

On your computer or mobile device, you can share files. Click on the three dots icon, it allows you to share files with everybody.

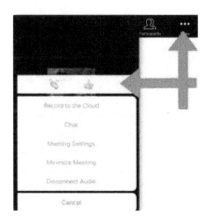

CONCLUSION

An electronic class will take place with the aid of networking technologies, at virtually no cost. Online classes are close to a traditional face-to-face class, particularly when one of the several software for conferences has been specially developed.

Within an online world, individuals can communicate with a community regardless of the physical position of the participants, or anyone can give a presentation or example when other participants are audience members. Video and audio technologies render electronic classes a professional option for alternative learning. Online classes work by using conference software that provides participants with services that imitate a face-to-face class. You will usually use a virtual system to deliver details using different resources – close to what one might use in a classroom. A whiteboard for the representation of points and sketches, a speech aspect that enables people either to speak to each other through a machine microphone or a conference telephone service and often via a text/chat function. Zoom can support video for this alternative learning option.

For starters, whether you operate from home using the apps for the internet and events, you'll communicate with peers or your students automatically. If you choose to fly, you can always sit down and engage in your colleagues' meetings or students' classes so that you do not lose crucial details, even though you're on the other side of the world!

The usage of electronic classes, as opposed to traditional, often increases time management. It takes time for everyone to assemble in the same place, sit down and talk. Everybody signs in at the same, designated time when you use conference software, and the class begins. There is less time to schedule an internet meeting because, for a certain number of participants, no tables or chairs need to be provided.

How do you decide which one is correct for you with several choices for electronic classes and internet conferences? You can browse the app for your requirements and find out how you are more likely to use it before signing up with one of the several organizations providing meeting services.

Are you going to hold daily regular classes or weekly maybe? Will you need to screen photos, or is there a whiteboard sufficiently to illustrate? Would you like to view certain programs through the meeting app on your computer? Some of the positive qualities of most online class service services are that you'll try the systems until you spend a subscription charge or purchase the product.

This helps you to check each of the apps for free, to decide whether the software fits your needs. After you have defined the possible uses for online gatherings, you'll decide the company that better serves the needs.

Zoom could be a savvy option, and much better for detailed discourse and making straightforward content notes. There's a whiteboard in the screen-sharing decisions that all members can expound on, and a 'break-out room' office where the educator will put understudies into little groups. Note that you'll require a paid record to make class-length brings with more than each understudy in turn, though for balanced reasons for existing, there's no such limitation.

www.ingramcontent.com/pod-product-compliance
Lightning Source LLC
La Vergne TN
LVHW051244050326
832903LV00028B/2562